I'm Saved! Now What? A Guide for Teens to go deeper with God will fill you with great encouragement and hope for our youth. Chantell Cooley's and Pastor Jp Wilson's book helps the reader totally surrender and know what to do with the questions they have about God and their spiritual walk. *I'm Saved! Now What?* is both spiritual and practical and a high recommend for leaders who work with youth. I believe God is going to send a great revival among the youth of America. To prepare for the outpouring, equip yourself with this must read book.

Dr. Marilyn Hickey
President—Marilyn Hickey Ministries

I'M SAVED! NOW WHAT?

A Guide for Teenagers To Go Deeper with God

How can a young person stay on the path of purity?
By living according to your word

(Psalm 119:9 NIV)

CHANTELL M. COOLEY, PASTOR JP WILSON

WestBow
PRESS
A DIVISION OF THOMAS NELSON

Copyright © 2012 by Chantell M. Cooley, Pastor Jp Wilson.

All rights reserved. No part of this book may be used or reproduced by any means, graphic, electronic, or mechanical, including photocopying, recording, taping or by any information storage retrieval system without the written permission of the publisher except in the case of brief quotations embodied in critical articles and reviews.

WestBow Press books may be ordered through booksellers or by contacting:

WestBow Press
A Division of Thomas Nelson
1663 Liberty Drive
Bloomington, IN 47403
www.westbowpress.com
1-(866) 928-1240

Because of the dynamic nature of the Internet, any web addresses or links contained in this book may have changed since publication and may no longer be valid. The views expressed in this work are solely those of the author and do not necessarily reflect the views of the publisher, and the publisher hereby disclaims any responsibility for them.

Any people depicted in stock imagery provided by Thinkstock are models, and such images are being used for illustrative purposes only.

Certain stock imagery © Thinkstock.

ISBN: 978-1-4497-6113-4 (sc)
ISBN: 978-1-4497-6115-8 (hc)
ISBN: 978-1-4497-6114-1 (e)

Library of Congress Control Number: 2012913526

Printed in the United States of America

WestBow Press rev. date: 08/21/2012

Introduction

Insights by Chantell

This is a book was inspired by God and the bible, and that inspiration was turned into a project by Pastor JP and myself. He was my youth pastor when I was sixteen years old. We have a burden to help young people go on and grow deep with God. We want you to know who you are in God and truly desire him more and more every day.

Pastor JP and I will be sharing our thoughts on the same topics but giving you two different perspectives. I will write to you from the point of view of a student in the Word and about how Pastor JP influenced me to grow deep in God. Pastor JP will write to you from the perspective of a youth pastor, giving you principles to follow just as he did with me when I was in his youth group.

In writing this book, we thought of all the ways we can help you get closer to God. We see many youth today who have had a great encounter with God. Maybe he has brought you back from a life of not serving him, or maybe you have accepted Jesus Christ in your heart for the first time. You might even feel like this is it and you want to really serve God all the way with no turning back.

If what you just read really hits home with you, then I am excited for you, because you are ready to dive deep into God's Word. I am living proof that the principles in the chapters to come will forever change your life. I put these principles into practice in my life when I was a teenager, and I have continued a strong walk with God.

I am blessed with Christian friends, and had good dating relationships that brought me a wonderful Christian husband. I went on to help my family in our business, which put me into positions of ownership that I never would have thought I could be in. God has placed so much favor on my life, and I know what I did as a teenager has caused my path to be full of blessings.

So now you might find yourself ready to do something for God, but you just don't know where to start. When you get saved, you are excited to begin something new. You have realized that your old life just was not the way to go. You might even find yourself facing new challenges as you become determined to really serve God with all your heart. All you know is that you have to have a Bible, and you have the desire to attend church.

You may be doing great on your walk with God, and then challenges come into your life that cause you to fall off a cliff and no longer think of God. Is that you sometimes? It happens to a lot of us. Staying on fire for God every day takes effort. I know many teenagers really want to give it a try, but for some reason they lose interest. Do you want to finally kick the desire to go back and forth?

Well, Pastor JP and I will reveal to you those very same principles he taught me when I was a teenager. We will get you excited about God and the plans he has for you. The Bible will become real to you as you learn to read it and put into practice what you've read. You will learn how to have time with God, and how he will answer your questions and guide you every day of your life.

Insights by Pastor JP

As Chantell stated, I was her youth pastor when she was in high school. I am now her pastor in a church in Foley, Alabama. I am amazed at what God has done through Chantell's life, just by Chantell's following the principles that I showed her many years ago. I know as you read the next chapters, God will cause you to be excited and full of anticipation about how you can be used in a mighty way.

A few days ago, one of our youth called me and asked if he could borrow some money. I said, "Why? What is going on?" He said that his car had run out of gas and he didn't have a way to get home. This reminds me of life. We can have the car, we can have the friends, and we can even have the destination—but if we do not have fuel, we will never arrive!

Life is like a recent event that happened to me. I entered a three-mile race with my wife. However, it was clear within just a few moments that I was not prepared for it. What started out as just a good Saturday morning bonding time with my wife and a few close friends turned into an experience that I had not thought out very well.

You see, for several months my beautiful wife jogged to prepare for this race. I would join her occasionally just to spend time with her, but would get bored pretty quickly. Eventually I would drop out and be at the house waiting for her by the time she was done.

When she invited me to run with her in the race, it seemed harmless. I looked at my schedule and didn't really have an excuse not to go, so I decided I would pacify her with a little brisk run and then get on with my day. Plus, she said, "You'll get a free T-shirt." That was it! Count me in!

What I didn't realize was that my wife, through her consistency and faithfulness in running, had built up quite a bit of stamina. Her pace had gotten faster than it had been the last time we jogged together.

On race day, there we were at the starting line, all huddled together with other runners. I was cracking jokes, laughing, and just enjoying the moment. Then I discovered that apparently someone had signed me up for the Olympics and had forgotten to tell me.

BANG! The gun went off in the middle of a joke I was telling. Suddenly it was as if I had gotten caught up in a mass of crazed shoppers on Black Friday at five in the morning. My wife grabbed my arm and shouted, "Run!"

She took off at a dead sprint. As if by instinct, I tried to catch her. She was still ten yards ahead of me after 200 yards, and I was already winded. I gasped, trying to stay with her amid shoulders and legs flying everywhere, asking her how long we were going to keep this pace.

She glanced back and exhorted me to man up and catch her. My pride feeling bruised, still somewhat confused as to what was happening, I found a couple ounces of energy and caught her. She looked over at me and no doubt saw a glimpse of death. She advised me that we had to keep up this pace for a mile.

I said, "*What?*" I informed her my heart was about to manifest itself visibly from within my T-shirt if we didn't slow down. I was baffled. I thought I had signed up for a little jog with my wife and friends. This was not looking anything like a jog. And where had my wife learned to run so fast? She seemed determined and locked into something that was beyond my comprehension.

I felt my legs screaming at me, and everything began to go downhill at once. A man of about seventy-five years old passed us. Looking ahead, I could see what appeared to be a boy of about twelve near the lead, showing no signs of slowing down.

That was it. I was doomed.

Determined not to quit, I did manage to utter some of the most painful words of my life to my wife: "You go on ahead, I've got to slow down." My male ego was on the grill and about to be consumed.

I slowed my pace just a little in order to spare my life and catch a breath. We crossed the two-mile marker, and I was thinking I might make it to the end without further damage when the ultimate humiliation came. A man pushing a kid in a stroller passed me by, not even breathing hard. *Seriously?*

That really was it. I had to admit that I had not been prepared for this race. I had no idea what I had gotten myself into. I finally made it to the end of the three-mile run, only to collapse on the ground as if I had been mortally wounded by a drive-by shooter.

I learned a huge lesson that day. I learned there is a difference between a marathon and a sprint. It was also another reminder that my walk with the Lord is very similar to that race. It lasts for a lifetime. It's serious. I had better approach my walk with the Lord in a very disciplined and thought-out way.

It is our hope that this book will give you a few pointers on the basics of a life lived for Christ. We have to be intentional about this race we are in.

After the race, when I had regained consciousness and natural breathing had come back to me, I had to make a confession to my wife. You see, when she told me she was going to start training for this race, she had immediately ordered some magazines about running. She literally began studying about running.

"Come on," I thought. "Is this really necessary? You can actually write books and articles about running?" I'd been running since I was a child and there didn't seem to be anything to write about. There was nothing to study; you just did it.

Guess what? I found out that I didn't know how to run. At least not how to run a race.

The apostle Paul in the Bible talks about living our lives as if we were running a race. If we're going to live our lives for Christ as if we were running a race, we really need to learn how to run.

When I think back about that race I ran with my wife, there was one thing that spared me. It was the water stations. Yes, to my surprise, they had people standing at tables handing out cups of water as I ran by. (Have you ever tried to run and drink at the same time? That's another story.)

Life requires refueling points that help us finish the race. This book is designed to give every young person daily fuel—things that will get them down the road to their purpose and destiny in Christ. I hope you enjoy the journey.

Chapter 1

FRIENDS

Insights by Chantell

The question I get many times from youth is about friends. Having the right friends is the first step to truly getting on the right track with God. A motivational speaker named Jim Rohn once said, "You are the average of the five people you spend the most time with." Think of the five closest friends you have and ask yourself: do you want to be like any one of those five people? Are they pushing you to be on fire for God? Are they thinking the way you think? Or are they pulling you back to your old ways?

I remember when I made the final break with the person who had been my best friend. I believe sometimes you test the waters for a while. You think you can have your old friends and do things you used to do, but still be a strong Christian. It is hard to truly follow after God with passion and still spend time with friends who don't share that same passion. They may go places that you used to want to go, but now you just don't feel like being around that crowd.

When I was a junior in high school, I was asked by my very good friend to go to a college campus to visit another friend. We planned to stay in the dorms and just hang out with the college age group and see the campus.

My mother was not really thrilled about this, but my dad thought it would be a good experience. I had no idea what to expect. I knew only a few students who had graduated from my high school the year before and were attending the college.

We finally arrived and got settled in our dorm. Following the lead of my friend, we got all dressed up. She was in charge of our night. It was like I was being led into the unknown. We walked to an area where a few people were gathered by their cars. Before I knew it, I was being asked to get into a guy's car. We were going somewhere that I didn't know. My friend sat in the back with another guy.

I panicked for a moment, realizing that I shouldn't be there.

The guy who was going to be driving leaned over and handed me a bottle of alcohol. I had never been offered anything like that before. Out of peer pressure, I took the bottle and drank a swallow from it. As I gave it back, I said to myself, "What are you doing? Oh my gosh, I don't want to be here. This is all wrong!"

Then I thought, "Before he starts the car, I need to jump out and go back to the dorm!" I had to make a split-second decision before he pulled out.

Thoughts were running through my head at lightning speed. I considered what everyone would think of me getting out of the car. I felt a lot of pressure to conform to their ways. I thought maybe if I just went along with them, it would be all right. But I felt God tugging at my heart to go—just go now, Chantell!

So I jumped out and told them I had to go. I gave them no time to question me, and ran so fast that there was no way anyone could catch me, much less talk me into staying. I just knew it was wrong!

Have you ever felt like that before? You were maybe at a party and just knew you were not supposed to be there? Maybe this guy you're dating wants to go all the way with you and you know you shouldn't?

Well, that feeling is the Holy Spirit telling you not to do it. Those small tugs at our hearts are God speaking to us and letting us know that if we listen to him, he will keep us out of harm. Honestly, there is no telling what would have happened to me if I had stayed in the car with that guy I had never seen before.

I am reminded of the story of Joseph and how he ran from temptation.

> Joseph was a strikingly handsome man. As time went on, his master's wife became infatuated with Joseph and one day said, "Sleep with me." He wouldn't do it. He said to his master's wife, "Look, with me here, my master doesn't give a second thought to anything that goes on here. He's put me in charge of everything he owns. He treats me as an equal. The only thing he hasn't turned over to me is you. You're his wife, after all!

How could I violate his trust and sin against God?" She pestered him day after day after day, but he stood his ground. He refused to go to bed with her. On one of these days, he came to the house to do his work and none of the household servants happened to be there. She grabbed him by his cloak, saying, "Sleep with me!" He left his coat in her hand and ran out of the house. (Genesis 39:6-14 MSG)

Notice that the Bible says that Joseph ran. He didn't walk; he ran! That is what I did that day. I ran as fast as I could from temptation.

The Devil wants to get you in a jam so you are forced to do something that you know in your heart you really don't want to do. The Bible says in James 4:7 (NIV), "Submit yourselves, then, to God. Resist the devil and he will flee from you."

Once I got back to the dorm room, I called my dad and said, "I just drank something, and I am done. I will never do this again." I just felt I had to confess and get my heart right again. Once I confessed it, I felt settled.

Sometimes you just have to get it out of your heart. You need to talk about what you did and then move on. I think it helps to heal your heart much faster than just holding it inside of you. If I had not called my dad that day, I would have exploded inside.

I wanted to go home at that point, but my friend wasn't about to go. It was party time, and I had left the scene. I really wasn't sure how I was going to get home. I hated to ask my parents to come and get me, so I prayed to God to show me what to do.

I started walking around the dorm, and I ran into a friend of mine who was visiting her brother. She lived right down the street from me, so I asked her if I could ride home with her. She said yes and that she was leaving the next morning. Can you believe that? God had answered my prayer.

As I packed up my things to go home, I thought, "You know, there is more to this life than getting into the party scene." It felt so empty and confused.

I know many teens who didn't make that split-second decision like I did. They think about what they're doing, and it really doesn't feel right to them, but they press on anyway to fit in. After a while, you simply keep going this way, and you might even be the life of the party. But I know that deep in your heart you feel empty, always wondering if there is more to life. I'm talking about something more fulfilling, something that has meaning and definition to it, rather than just drinking, smoking pot, doing drugs, or having sex before marriage.

Anyway, my friend and I were a few miles from our street when the car went out of control. She put on her brakes really quickly, and we started spinning in the middle of the road. I saw a blur of trees as we went around several times. I was stuck in shock with a blank stare on my face; I couldn't even get out a scream. I thought we would never stop spinning around, but the car finally came to a stop in the middle of the road.

My friend and I just looked at each other, and I knew God had his angels working on the scene. The Devil wanted to kill me that day. He knew once I got hold of God that I would never turn back, but move forward and help other friends, too.

Moving On with God

From that day forward, I vowed to stay focused on God and be a true Christian. I started to go to a youth group at the church that my parents attended. I really didn't like it, but it was a start.

I asked the friend who'd invited me to the college campus to go to this youth group with me, but she decided not to go with me. When I decided not to party, it really put a label on me that I wasn't any fun. I mean, we were still friends in the hallways of school, but it wasn't the same. I knew that I could not lead two lives. I had to make a decision to get fully involved with a youth group and stay connected with God. I know when you make these decisions that it's not the easiest thing to do. You really don't want to lose your old friends, but sometimes that happens.

God Moves in New Friends

There was a period of time during this year that I was very alone. I started reading my Bible, and the Scripture verse that helped me was Jeremiah 29:11 (NIV), "For I know the plans I have for you, declares the Lord, plans to prosper you and not to harm you, plans to give you a hope and a future." I also read different books about how to keep focused on God and how to read the Bible.

I prayed that God would bring me Christian friends. I declared to God what kind of friends I wanted to have in my life. As I looked at my school, I didn't see any potential friends who believed as I did. What I did know was God had a plan for me.

God is bigger than this problem of not having friends. I think sometimes that when you make a change in your life, I mean really make the cut, that God allows you to be just you and him for a while. There was a period of about three months that I had no friends. During that time, I just hung out with my family and played basketball with the school team.

But one day I was sitting on the bleachers at the football field. It was science fair day, and all the students were outside for a time. I was alone and reading a book.

Well one day, this girl came up to me and said, "Hi, what are you reading?"

I am sure I froze and stumbled with my words because I had to say it was a Christian book. I was preparing to be put down by her. To my surprise, she was excited about what I was reading. She said she was a Christian and shared with me that she was reading a Christian book as well. She explained that not too long ago, she had let her friends go as well, and she was alone.

That day, she invited me to attend her youth group. There I met her youth pastor, JP Wilson.

God Knows Exactly What You Need

God knows what you need at the exact time you need it. I was diligent in my walk with God, keeping myself busy and staying away from the party scene. All of a sudden, out of the blue, God brought me a friend who is still my friend to this day, and we both are sold out to God.

So if you find yourself in the same situation as me, hang in there. God will show up right when you need him. Remember the Scripture verse that helped me? Jeremiah 29:11. Write it on a notecard and put it in your binder so while you are at school, you can remind yourself that God knows exactly what you need. The verse says, "For I know the plans I have for you, declares the Lord, plans to prosper you and not to harm you, plans to give you hope and a future. (Jer. 29:11 NIV) I know that day God did give me a hope and a future through a special friend.

Life is partly what we make it and partly what it is made by the friends we choose. Choosing friends who build you up and believe the way you believe truly makes a difference. I talk to many youth who choose to part ways with old friends. I hear many stories where students have had a life-changing experience, maybe on a mission trip or at a youth retreat, and their friends did not come with them. These students go back to school charged up and wanting to start fresh, but are faced with friends who don't get what God has done.

A Senior in High School

This story is about a guy who had a great experience on the mission field. He came back a different person. He told his friends that he didn't want to party. He invited them to come to youth group with him and experience what he had experienced. Some came with him, while others didn't like this new person he was becoming.

He mentioned to me that it is really hard to walk down the hallways and pass your friends as they are laughing and smiling, and realize you are not in their lives any longer. You always have in the back of your mind that you are missing out on something. Maybe you aren't getting invited to the movies as you always were, or maybe your once-best friend has replaced you with other people, and you are all alone.

At this point, you come to an important time in your walk with God. This is where you can either let temptation cause you to go back to your old ways, or you can carve out a new path. Take a stand and let your friends know that what you used to do is not a good lifestyle for you, and that you are much happier now than you have ever been.

You can share with them the change in your life and ask them to come with you to youth events and church. Your friends might question you and decide to come with you to check it out, or they may make it known to you that this "Jesus thing" is not for them. I encourage you to move forward. Don't let anyone make you feel like you are the one who made the wrong choice.

I am reminded of Psalm 107:20 (MSG), which says, "He spoke the word that healed you, that pulled you back from the brink of death." This means that God healed your heart. Maybe you have been hurt by things from your past. Maybe you never felt loved, or you did some things that you are not proud of. But you've made the decision to let God in your heart, and he is healing you now.

God will lift you up and help you make the right decisions. He will not leave you alone, but will be by your side as you face these challenges.

God Is with You Always

Joshua 1:9 (NIV) says, "For the Lord your God will be with you wherever you go." In this new journey, God will direct your every step if you will let him.

Just let go and say this prayer out loud:

God, my old ways were not working out for me, but I want to move on with you. I take that chance because I know you will direct my steps. You will bring the right friends in my life. I am ready to move on, and I resist temptations to go back to my old ways. In Jesus' name, amen.

Give God Time to Work

I think many times we don't give God a chance to bring new friends into our lives. Maybe we don't let God use us to bring our old friends to him. We are so scared of what people will say about us that we don't allow God to work.

So I encourage you to stay focused on God. As the Scripture says, "Steep your life in God-reality, God-initiative, God-provisions. Don't worry about missing out. You'll find all your everyday human concerns will be met" (Matthew 6:33 MSG). What this passage is saying is to make that stand. Be God-focused. Don't look to the right or the left. Just visualize yourself putting one foot in front of the other. Take initiative to tell others about why you are so excited about God and how he can be applied to your everyday life.

God Begins to Use You

When I was in school, I started attracting friends as I got more bold about who I was in God. Before I knew it, I had new friends wanting to come to church. I had a following of friends who wanted to feel the same way I felt. They had hurts and mistakes, and they wanted a clean slate.

I always tell youth that when you get excited about God, you get contagious. Everyone starts wanting what you have. As you share, your faith gets stronger. When friends you once had tell you that you are stupid or a Jesus freak, you can say, "I am a Christian, and I am proud of it."

You become confident in yourself. You will have other friends who can back you up. You know in your heart this is the real thing.

Standing Up for God

Being a Christian in junior high or high school is a great thing. Be excited about your youth group and church. You will get more respect for taking a stand and saying the word no. Many who see you will wish they could make this stand and will want to go down the path you are going down. They will ask you, "What has changed you?" and "How did you say or do that in front of everyone? How are you not giving in to temptations?" This will be your chance to share with them why you did this and how you are different.

My son and his cousin are both in high school. They stay God-focused and have reputations for not cussing and for being friendly to everyone around. They both are very wise about the friends they choose and know not to get caught with others who only think of ungodly things. They made a stand for their beliefs in God and didn't worry about being put down. They both have made a stand for God, and respect follows them. They are highly favored and stand out as the ones to follow. God is using them to lead their school for God.

Insights from Pastor JP

What every young person wants is a friend. The idea of being alone is almost more than any young person can bear.

I once heard a person say, "Be very grateful if you live your life and experience two genuine friendships." Truth is, people rarely experience genuine friendships early in life. Why? Because in their teen years, most people are just trying to figure out who they are and what they want to do in life. Their lives are really mostly "about them."

As a child, I remember watching a TV show about a soldier willing to be captured by enemy forces and left behind by his unit if he could just have a little more time to protect some kids he had fallen in love with at a local orphanage. He grieved over the choice he was forced to make: stay or go. Eventually he chose others over himself. That is what genuine love is. You choose to put yourself second in order to help someone else.

Laying Down Your Life

That TV show made a big impression on me. The soldier watched the American helicopter leave while he held a little child in his arms. He was truly trading in his freedom for a life of hardship and personal danger. God, for a brief moment, opened my eyes to what it truly means to lay down one's life for a brother.

I went into our living room, knelt down at a chair, and cried for several hours. At ten years of age, I asked God to give me a love for people. Love for what he loved.

After a while, the strangest thing happened. I found myself praying for all of my classmates. I named them one by one. I asked God to save them like he had saved me. Then something came out of my mouth that stunned even me—a petition, if you will. I heard myself saying, "God, even if I have to lose all my friends in order to point them to you, I'm willing to do it!"

I almost could not believe what I was saying, but I sure felt it. I genuinely wanted my friends to experience what I had begun to experience. Love. The reality of a life lived in God.

From that point on, my relationship with my friends changed. Why, you might ask? Because I had changed. God had opened my little-boy eyes and heart to see that my classmates needed Jesus. The thought that I might be the only way they could ever meet him became a game-changer for me.

Later, I read about something Jim Elliott said before he died a martyr at age twenty-nine. He was killed at the hands of savage cannibals in South America when he tried to reach out to them as a missionary. He said, "A man cannot keep what he did not earn to gain what he did not lose." It dawned on me that my journey could end up being a lonely one. I realized I might lose many friends who would not want what I had to offer. That thought scared me, yet did I really have a choice?

It was settled in my heart. I knew what I had to do.

I started by asking my friends and classmates if they knew Jesus. That seems elementary, but it's where the change starts. So many are afraid to ask that simple little question.

Stepping Out for God

My little boy and I were riding down the road the other day when he told me how many Christians were in his class. I found it kind of odd that my son would know something like this. So I asked him how he knew. "Simple, Dad. I just asked them."

Have you asked your friends if they know Jesus? If not, then why haven't you? Is it because you feel embarrassed or fearful they will call you a Jesus freak? Maybe they'll exclude you from some things if you look to be going a little overboard about this Jesus thing. But do you really have a choice?

I remember inviting a classmate of mine to church when I was sixteen. I picked him up, took him to church, and then drove him home. We were silent as we went back to his house. I was a little hesitant to ask him how he liked church.

When he was getting out, I asked him, "Mike, you want me to pick you up next week to go to church again?"

He bent down, looked at me, and said, "Don't you ever ask me to go to something as ridiculous as that again!"

With that, he slammed the car door shut and walked to his house. I remember driving off feeling rejected, discouraged, and lonely. I had lost another potential friend.

Eight years later, I got a call. It was Mike. He said, "JP, I had to call you. I wanted you to be the first to know. I've asked Jesus into my heart! This is the greatest thing that has ever happened to me!"

Then he said something shocking to me. "JP, this is so good. Why didn't you beat me up or something to convince me of how great this is?"

Wow. Can you believe that?

You see, you're just a witness. You're not the one on trial—Jesus is. If a judge were to ask me to be a witness for a legal case, I would take the stand and testify about the person who was on trial. If the jury decided to reject my testimony, it really would have no effect on me. I would still live my life. Why? Because I wouldn't be the one they were making a judgment against.

Let me say this. If you are truly to find a great friend, you will find him or her not because you are looking for a friend, but because you are looking for Jesus.

Choosing to be Happy with God

One time in college I was really bummed out. My roommate asked me the cause of my moping around in the apartment. I told him I didn't have a girlfriend.

I will never forget his response. He taught me one of the most important truths I have ever learned in my life. He said, "JP, you'll never be happy with someone until you've learned how to be happy without someone."

What? I thought having relationships with people would fulfill me but if you don't have a relationship with God you will still feel empty and unsatisfied. I had to think about his words for a while. I've come to know they are true.

I'm not advocating that we have no friends, and I'm certainly not saying we should not want friends. However, I am saying that until you have learned to be completely happy without a friend, then you'll always be a taker and not a giver. People will be the source of your happiness. In a sense, your need for people will replace your need for God.

I was at the mall the other day and saw a girl sitting on a bench by herself, just texting away. I saw a boy standing with some other boys, but he was too busy talking on his phone to talk to his companions. It seemed to me that the ability to communicate had been forgotten.

Then an event took place which explained it all to me. Our youth group decided to do a fund-raiser. Our job was to park cars and then direct traffic for a big community event. I was stationed with a youth at a strategic location. When the event was over, we were supposed to stop traffic and escort the pedestrians across the road. When the pedestrians started walking toward us, however, I noticed my help was gone.

Later, I saw him off to the side, texting away. When the pedestrians were gone, I went over and asked the texting teen, "What are you doing? Why did you leave me high and dry at our command post?"

His reply was, "I didn't want to look all those people in the eye." In other words, his desire to give got lost in his fear of people.

When you're in love with Jesus, you lose your need to fill your unstructured time or awkward moments with your phone, texting, or Facebooking. You can be happy just by yourself. Reading a book that encourages your walk with God or reading your Bible might even completely satisfy that emptiness you have for a boyfriend or girlfriend.

My point is simply this: are you willing to go it alone? Not that you will, but you may. Are you okay when it's just you and Jesus?

Questions on Friendships:

Take time to ask yourself these questions. Ask God to help you. Be strong as you make a stand for God.

* Name three things your present friendships have done to draw you closer to God.

* How many times have you heard your friends tell someone else about Jesus?

* Do your friends enjoy talking about other people's flaws?

* How do your friends talk to their moms and dads?

* Do your friends ever ask you what you've been reading in the Bible or what you've been reading in your devotion?

* What do your friends do on the weekend?

* What kinds of pictures are on your friends' Facebook profiles?

* What do your friends post on Twitter?

Fuel Stop:

Now is the time to get your notebook out and write out the Scripture verses on the next page. By doing this, you are putting them in your heart. Say them over in your everyday life. When you speak them, you are agreeing with God that they are true and will work in your life. My daughter writes them on notecards and puts them in her notebook so she can be reminded of them all day long.

Scripture verses to think about:

One who has unreliable friends soon comes to ruin, but there is a friend who sticks closer than a brother. (Proverbs 18:24 NIV).

Be kind and compassionate to one another, forgiving each other, just as in Christ God forgave you. (Ephesians 4:32 NIV)

How can a young person stay on the path of purity? By living according to your word. (Psalm 119:9 NIV).

The righteous chose their friends carefully, but the way of the wicked leads them astray. (Proverbs 12:26 NIV).

For I know the plans I have for you, declares the Lord, plans to prosper you and not to harm you, plans to give you hope and a future. (Jeremiah 29:11 NIV).

He sent out his word and healed them; He rescued them from the grave. (Psalm 107:20 NIV).

Have not I commanded you? Be strong and courageous. Do not be afraid; do not be discouraged, for the Lord your God will be with you wherever you go. (Joshua 1:9 NIV).

But seek first his kingdom and his righteousness, and all these things will be given to you as well. (Matthew 6:33 NIV).

Chapter 2

BIBLE

Insights from Pastor JP

When I was a boy, I developed the desire to read in a weird way—not because I enjoyed it, but because that was all there really was to do.

Don't get me wrong. I was a typical boy who loved playing sports and hacking away in the great outdoors. Building tree houses, swimming in the creek, and ice-skating were my ideas of fun. Sitting silently in a chair to focus on words on a page had its challenges until I started riding the school bus.

I rode the bus every morning for more than an hour and every night for another hour and a half. There is only so much sightseeing you can do before you're ready to jump out the window. Forced to find other ways to occupy my time, I decided to read a book. Seriously? Yes, a book.

I chose a biography, believe it or not. It didn't take me long to become fascinated with the lives of ordinary men who did extraordinary things. Somehow I would be sucked in to their real-life situations, incredible sacrifices, and unexpected rewards. I remember allowing my imagination to take me back in time. In my mind I hunted with Daniel Boone, fought with George Custer, grieved with Abraham Lincoln, and escaped from shackles with Harry Houdini. The next thing I knew, it would be time to get off the bus.

I challenge you to do the same thing. Get lost in someone else who lived a great life. But this time I must move you to get sucked in to the life of the most incredible person ever to walk this planet. This was a person whose kindness overshadowed Mother Teresa and whose bravery surpassed William Wallace. His insights dwarfed Albert Einstein, and his leadership skills left Winston Churchill in the dust.

In fact, the one of whom I speak was adored by the likes of George Washington, Martin Luther King Jr., Samuel Adams, and Michelangelo. They read about and studied the life of this individual. They memorized his words, dissected his movements, and patterned their lives after this one person. Their greatest desire, along with those of millions of others, was to somehow be compared to him.

Why? Because this person seemed to do no wrong to anyone. He had a way of turning tragedies into triumphs, dead ends into highways, and sorrow into joy. The multitudes followed him for miles, even going without food if they had to just to catch the next speech, message, or lesson. Those words captivated the hearts of little children while confounding the minds of the most intelligent. His way of living seemed strange to some but somehow compelling to all. He truly was amazing. In fact, stories about this person are still being told today all over the world. People continue to study him in hopes of bettering their own lives.

Why? Because this person truly brought *life* to you. I mean that literally and figuratively. No other person has had a way of speaking words that, when put into practice, changed people's lives for the good. I mean *way* good!

Reading the Bible

Who is this person? His name is Jesus.

So what am I trying to say?

Read the book describing his life. Know this man named Jesus, who never did anything wrong, and try to figure out how to be like him.

Start by reading the gospel of John. The Bible is divided into two parts, the Old Testament and the New Testament. Everything in the Old Testament happened before Jesus came to earth. Everything in the New Testament happened from Jesus' time forward.

The gospel of John is located in the New Testament. In fact, it's the fourth book of the New Testament. This gospel very clearly documents Jesus' life from birth to death. It will take you on a journey all the way from his supernatural birth to his amazing demonstration of love on a little hill called Calvary, where he hung on a cross. You will enjoy watching this amazing individual navigate through life with wisdom and determination. He will blow you away by the things he says and does.

What's even more amazing is that he will turn around after he has left you speechless and say, "Greater things than these shall *you* do!" How could it get much better?

Old and New Testaments

Another thing that's interesting to me is that they called the parts of the Bible the Old and New Testaments. Think about that. Do you know what a testament is?

When a person dies, many times a lawyer will call family and friends in to read for them the last will and testament written by the deceased person. It is a proclamation of what has been left as an inheritance. When you read the Bible, you're finding out what things have been left to you as your inheritance.

Honestly, only a fool would not care to know what his inheritance is. Who knows what you would be missing out on by not reading the will? The Bible is full of promises that have been guaranteed to you. They are your rights. They are your privileges. They are things you are entitled to. We call them promises. Every Christian has a right to claim these promises as her or his own. All you have to do is read the Bible and then confess it.

At the end of each chapter of this book, we have given you a list of Scripture passages that you can start confessing. By doing this, you will allow the Word to come alive and do in your life what it says it will do. Then just keep watching, waiting, and believing in its manifestation, because it's coming your way.

Wow! That's good news. In fact that's what we call the message Jesus preached—the gospel. The word gospel means good news. Who wouldn't want to immerse themselves in the Good News?

Insights from Chantell

What is the purpose of a Bible?

As a teenager, I noticed the first thing people asked me when I got saved was, "Do you have a Bible?" I can remember looking for my Bible in my nightstand drawers. I always had a Bible, but I really didn't understand the purpose of it. Everyone said, "Bring your Bible with you," but what were we going to do with this Bible? Why was it important? Would I ever want to read the Bible? It just seemed so uninteresting to me.

There is something about the Bible that causes you to feel attached to it. Maybe you don't know why you feel this way, but you just know it gives you peace and maybe even comforts you. I can remember when I was in high school, there were times when I took my Bible to school. It was a small leather Bible. I would put it in my locker, and if I had free time, I would read it. There were many times I would sleep with my Bible. If I was going through some rough times in my life, it comforted me. I knew that everything was going to work out as long as I had my Bible with me.

Going Deeper with God

I was talking to a group of students who were in eighth through twelfth grade. It was a mixed group of guys and girls. This group wanted to go deeper with God. What I mean by that is they didn't just want to be average Christians. They wanted to know more about the Bible and how they could defeat the enemy every day.

I told them to bring their Bibles, pens, and notebooks to help them grow deeper with God. These are the keys to your journey with God. It's like building a house: the first thing you have to put down are the stakes that outline the house. Only then is the foundation poured.

Pastor JP taught me to read the Bible and take notes on what I read. As I did this, the Bible really came alive to me. You know when you read something, and you think, "That's for me!" Like that sentence was talking right to you. That is how the Word, which is the Bible, works for you and me. We can take a Scripture verse, dissect it, and figure out how it applies to our lives.

Different Versions of the Bible

There are many different versions of the Bible written for us now. The original text of the Bible was written in many languages, such as Aramaic and Greek. Different translators have created different "versions" of that original text in English.

How does that work? Well, think of the different words you use every day to refer to the same thing. You might call the place you live "my house," "my home," "my crib," or just "my place," depending on who you were speaking to and what mood you were in.

In the same way, a translator can choose from many different words in English to express an idea found in the original text. The version of the Bible that you prefer will often depend upon how you feel about the translator's choice of words. But all versions of the Bible are translated from the same source and express the same ideas. Personally, I like the New International version, the Amplified version, and the Message version. My kids really love their Message Bible because they feel it is more like the way they talk every day. You have to decide what version you like.

There are many Bible apps you can download for free on your smartphone or computer. Apps help you jump back and forth to view different versions. Sometimes you read a verse and you just don't understand what it is saying to you. You can go to another version of the Bible to see the same verse expressed in another way. Here's an example from Psalm 138:8.

> The Lord will perfect that which concerns me; Your mercy and loving-kindness, O Lord, endure forever—forsake not the works of Your own hands (*Amplified Bible*, or AB).

> Finish what you started in me, God. Your love is eternal—don't quit on me now (*The Message: The Bible in Contemporary Language*, or MSG).

> The Lord will vindicate me: your love, Lord, endures forever—do not abandon the works of your hands (*New International Version*, or NIV).

> Jehovah will perfect that which concerneth me: Thy lovingkindness, O jehovah, endureth

for ever; Forsake not the works of thine own hands (*American Standard Version*, or ASV).

One Scripture verse is communicated in four different ways by using different words. For example, the Amplified version goes into more detail, which may help you to understand the verse better.

How can we apply this verse to our lives? I like the Amplified version best for this verse because it says, "The Lord will perfect that which concerns me." That is saying to me that whatever is going on in my life at that moment, God will make it perfect.

It could be that you are not getting along with your parents, and there are issues causing you to want to leave the situation. Maybe you just broke up with your boyfriend or girlfriend; you feel lost and are not sure what to do next. The verse tells us that God will come upon the scene and make a new way for you. You probably can't see how this situation could get better, but Scripture says that the Lord will perfect that which concerns you. God's Word is alive, and he will perform that which was spoken.

If you have a situation in your life that is just not turning out the way you planned, well, write this verse on an index card and speak it out loud over your life every day. Say it just like this:

> The Lord will perfect that which concerns me today. This situation in my life will be made perfect according to Psalm 138:8. Thank you, God, that you will make all situations turn out just right today.

What you are doing is making that Scripture promise your own. You are confessing it and causing the Word to work in your life.

Meditate on the Word

In Joshua 1:8, it says to meditate on the word day and night so that you will make your way prosperous. "Meditate" means to think or to dwell upon. This passage does not say to meditate one day a week or maybe a couple times a week—it says day and night.

What that is telling me that you need to write down a Scripture verse that speaks to you, and then read it as much as you can. Put it in your notebook. Meditate on it.

As you read your Bible, you are meditating on God's Word, and it will begin to work in your life. I know that if you meditate on Psalm 138:8, the situations in your life will be perfected.

Standing Up for God

God's word is safety for us as well. Let me explain.

When I was a senior in high school, everyone knew that I was a Christian and that I was not ashamed to show it. I was the president of the Fellowship of Christian Athletes, and we planned to put up signs in the hallways promoting our meetings. So I asked a couple of guys to get poster board and write on it about the next meeting. They put the board up, and I went about my day.

At midmorning, the bell rang for break. I came out of class and noticed a big group of students standing by the water fountain. I went over to see what all the confusion was about and noticed that the poster board I had told the guys to put up was above the water fountain. But there was something new written down in the corner. It said, "Jesus is Dead!"

I was in shock. Even as I tell this story now, I get the chills. I thought, "How dare you say that about my God?"

There were all different groups of students standing around. Many were very popular. At least twenty students were there, waiting to see what would happen next. The person who had defaced the poster was still standing by the water fountain with the pen in his hand. He had a trench coat on and was viewed as a Satanist at our school.

Thoughts rushed through my mind: I would be called a Jesus freak or this guy might try to hurt me if I stood up to him. But then I thought, "If you call yourself a Christian, then stand up for God. He stood up for you and died on the cross. You can at least do this for him." At that moment, I told myself I would not let the guy in the trench coat do this.

I pushed through the crowd and made my way to the front. I went up to the sign. I looked the guy in the face. Then I crossed out the word "dead" and wrote "alive" above it. I said, "Jesus is alive and not dead!" I looked the guy straight in the eyes. I felt like I was staring at Satan himself.

We stood there looking at each other, and I can assure you I felt scared and brave all at the same time. He proceeded to mark out "alive" and wrote "dead" again!

I thought, "Oh my gosh, I can't believe this!" This guy was in my art class, so he saw me reading my devotion or Bible during class sometimes. He and I would go back and forth about my beliefs and his beliefs daily.

I immediately crossed out "dead" again and wrote "ALIVE" really big.

No one in the crowd was saying a word. It was like time stood still.

About that time the bell rang, and he just left along with everyone else. I stood there smiling and saying to myself, "I won!"

God is alive! God rose up in me and helped me. He perfected that which concerned me. God's Word worked for me that day.

Questions on the Bible:

Take time to ask yourself these questions. Ask God to help you. Be strong as you make a stand for God.

*   Do I have a daily schedule to read the Bible?

*   What version of the Bible do I have?

*   What is the purpose of reading the Bible for my life?

*   What three things do you see in Jesus' life that are not present in yours?

*   How can you begin to add these traits in your life?

Fuel Stop:

Set up a schedule to read the Bible. Start with the gospel of John. Have your notebook and pen ready to write down verses as you read, and God will give you understanding of the Word.

Find a friend who wants to get into the Bible like you do. Ask that friend to become your prayer partner. Ask him or her to hold you accountable for reading every day. Have your prayer partner ask you about the Word you are striving for every week at youth group, church, or school.

Scripture verses to think about:

The Lord will perfect that which concerns me; Your mercy and loving-kindness, O Lord, endure forever—forsake not the works of Your own hands. (Psalm 138:8 AMP).

The Book of the Law shall not depart out of your mouth, but you shall meditate on it day and night, that you may observe and do according to all that is written in it. For then you shall make your way prosperous, and then you shall deal wisely and have good success (Joshua 1:8 AMP).

The lions may grow weak and hungry, but those who seek the Lord lack no good thing. (Psalm 34:10 NIV).

Every place on which the sole of your foot treads, I have given it to you, just as I spoke to Moses. (Joshua 1:3 AMP).

Chapter 3

PRAYER

Insights from Pastor JP

Prayer. What exactly is this? Most everyone does it at some point in their lives, but why? What is its purpose?

Prayer is simply what we call communicating with God. It's about you talking to God and God talking back to you. That's it! Simple, don't you think? It can be done anywhere at any time. If you are on a subway, plane, or boat, you can pray. God is always listening. If you are about to step into the batter's box, eat a sandwich, or take a test, it makes no difference; you can pray. You can do it out loud, silently, or in between. Any way and anyhow, God loves to hear you talk to him.

I remember talking to some young people about prayer once, and they were telling me how hard it was for them. I asked them what the problem seemed to be. They said, "We usually fall asleep, get distracted, or are just plain bored."

I asked them if they got bored when they were talking to their boyfriends or girlfriends. They said, "Of course not!"

I asked them, "Well, why not?"

They said, "Because we love them and are interested in them. We can see them, and furthermore we can hear them."

"Well," I said, "I know you love God and are interested in him, and I'm confident you can see evidence of him all around, even though you may not physically see him."

But seeing isn't an issue either; Helen Keller and Fanny Crosby, two very famous blind people, had the capability to believe and love.

"It sounds like your biggest problem is that you're just not hearing," I said, and they agreed.

Hearing the Voice of God

I explained to these students that hearing is something you have to acquire. You literally have to learn the voice of God. You don't typically wake up hearing God. Of course you may have dreams influenced by the Lord. Or someone you trust may say they have a word for you from God. But how do you hear God yourself? You train yourself to hear.

When my son was quarterbacking his football team, I heard the coach say, "Boy, when you are in the game, you don't listen to anybody but me. I'm going to call the plays. You must stay focused on me in order to execute the call. Do you understand?" Basically what that coach was telling my son was that the coach's voice had to be distinguished above all other voices. There were times when my son couldn't see the coach, but he could hear that voice above everyone else's voice, and thus knew what to do.

I went to a wrestling tournament once and saw two boys wrestling with each other. They were so involved in the match they had no time to stand and look at their coaches. Yet while they were wrestling, they were each listening to one voice above all the others. Not the voices of parents or friends, but the voice of the coach sending instructions their way.

Learning the Voice of God

It is vital that you learn the voice of your heavenly coach. Only he knows the next move you need to make as you walk this life. At times you will find yourself wrestling with your own carnal desires or even fighting against unseen spiritual forces. Hearing your coach is extremely important. With his voice resonating in your ear, you will never find yourself with your guard down. You have the greatest coach in the universe, and he knows you like the back of his hand. He knows you can win and how that can happen in your life. All you need to do is learn his voice and desire to hear it.

Perhaps you've had this happen to you: you met someone, exchanged phone numbers, and later got a call from that new acquaintance. Did you recognize the voice at first? Well, probably not. Why? Because you hadn't been around that person long enough to recognize her or his voice. You probably had to ask who was calling several times before you became more familiar with that voice. However, there comes a point in any relationship when the other person no longer has to identify himself. You just know who it is by the sound of the voice.

It's the same with God. No one knows God's voice at first. Why? Because most of the time it's not an audible voice. In my life, I've only heard an audible voice once, but I've heard God speak to me hundreds of times. How? It's like a thought that brings incredible peace to me. Many times it is totally contrary to what my flesh wants to do, but it brings a settling deep within my gut.

I've tested these thoughts by stepping out and acting on them or against them. I've learned to distinguish between my thoughts and his thoughts.

Changing Your Prayer Time with God

When you really believe that God wants to hear you and longs to talk to you, then your prayer time starts to change. You look forward to praying because you believe he is going to talk to you. I would be bored if every time I went to talk to my friend, he just stared at me and never said a word. God is not like that. He talks and communicates to his kids.

That's right. We're his kids and he is our Father.

That never became any more real to me than when I was praying for a financial need. I didn't have enough money to pay my bills. I didn't know what else to do, so I decided to pray.

I went to a room, shut the door, and began worshipping the Lord. I mean, that's important to do before you start asking God for stuff. You need to tell him how great he is and brag on him out loud. Why? Not because he is on an ego trip, but because you need to humble yourself and remember it's not all about you.

So I worshipped and sang praises to God before I asked him to provide some funds to pay my bill. Then I heard God speak. It was a thought in the form of a reproach. He said, "You really don't believe I'm listening. You don't believe I will do this for you."

What he said next made me stop in my footsteps. He said, "I am not like your earthly father. I am unlike any father you have ever known. Quit comparing me to him. I am the heavenly Father, and I do listen. I care, and I will help you."

You can imagine my sense of humiliation mixed with joy from this divine rebuke I had experienced.

I want you to know you can hear God's voice, and he wants to talk to you. Begin now to train your ear for his voice and only his voice. Watch incredible things happen from this point on.

Insights from Chantell

By now you should have a good foundation of understanding about why you need strong Christian friends and why you need to read the Bible. These two things are essential in staying focused on God.

Have you ever seen people who are fired up for God one week, and then the next it's like they are back to the old people they used to be? See, the Devil wants to steal you back as fast as he can. He knows if you really get God in your heart and understand that you were put on this earth to bring others to God—well, then Satan would be in trouble. He will do everything he can to win you back over.

Satan is a liar and manipulator. Have you ever had a friend who says one thing and then goes behind your back and says another thing? That is what the Devil wants to do to you. He wants to remind you of all the things you used to do and convince you that you are missing out on all the "fun." He knows that "fun" is all too often another word for sin, but he's not going to admit that to you.

Prayer Will Defeat the Devil

The one thing Pastor JP taught me that has always and will continue to defeat the Devil in my life is prayer. Praying over your life daily is essential in keeping yourself full of God. When you see your friends just drift off and not stay on track with God, it means they are forgetting to bring prayer into their lives. Pastor JP taught me that building in time to pray in the morning or at night will build me up and keep the Devil off my case.

While I was in the youth group, Pastor JP said that he wanted to start a prayer team every morning. This was during the summer months, and we had to be at the church by 6:30 a.m. as many mornings as we could come. A couple of my best friends, would come and pick me up in the early morning hours, and off we would go to the church to pray. I can remember a couple of times I overslept. They said they stood knocking at my door for a few minutes and left. That only happened twice because I felt I just missed God. I would finally wake up and realize I overslept and I was in the worst mood the rest of the day. It became so important to start my day off with God praying and seeking him early that morning.

It was a huge sacrifice to do this. But we wanted all God could give us, and we knew that praying was helping us have better days. We would gather in a big room and thank God for all the things he had done and was going to do for our lives. Also, I would thank him for how wonderful he is and to worship him.

I know many times that I dozed off for a few minutes and then picked back up. I stumbled, but continued to intercede over my life, my friends' lives, and the lives of my family.

God Wants to Hear Our Praises

You know God wants to hear our praises to him. It honors him, and it gets the focus off ourselves and onto him. When I praise God, I visualize all of me coming out of my body, and that body filling up with God. I wanted to be led by God and not by me. I get myself in trouble and make wrong decisions, but with God in me, I can be led by him.

In 1 Thessalonians 5:17 (AB), it says, "Be unceasing in prayer [praying perseveringly]." In the Message version, it says, "Pray all the time."

"So," you might ask, "how do I do that?" Well, you can pray in your car as you go to school or work, and also pray as you are getting ready for school.

You might ask, "Well, what do I say?" Begin by thanking God for all he has done for you. Then you can petition him with problems or concerns you have, in your life or in others' lives.

Pray Over Your School

I would always park my car by the gym at school and walk to class. I had to go through the middle school grounds to get to the high school. On my way, I would begin to pray over my school. God gave me a heart to change my school. I touched the buildings and believed that those inside would desire God and receive all that God had for them. I prayed that God would convict their hearts and cause them to not to want to party and drink any longer.

I remember after school was over one afternoon, I stayed to pray over the lockers. I walked up and down the halls praying for a revival in my school. I prayed there would be new kids raised up like me who wanted God in their school and wanted to see something great happen.

That kind of prayer is powerful! Prayer brings change in situations. It might take time, but prayer is the key to unlocking situations that you think will never change.

I am reminded of Luke 11:9 (AMP), "So I say to you, Ask and keep on asking and it shall be given you; seek and keep on seeking and you shall find; knock and keep on knocking and the door shall be opened to you." This verse tells you to keep on praying and asking God to help you and to intervene in situations.

Dating and Relationships

One of the things I think every teenager needs to pray over is relationships, especially with other teens. Almost every conversation I have with a teen leads to wanting a girlfriend or boyfriend. I always begin the conversation with the question, "Have you prayed over this to see if this is right for your life?"

God loves friendships and relationships, but these relationships need to be uplifting and encouraging you, not bringing you down or steering you away from God's perfect will for your life.

If you want that special guy in your life, you need to constantly pray for God to guide you to strong Christian friends who will help and encourage you to grow deeper in God. Ephesians 5:17 (MSG) says, "Don't live carelessly unthinkingly. Make sure you understand what the Master wants."

So, you say, how am I supposed to know what God wants? My answer to you is prayer. Spending time with God and getting to know him will cause his desires to become your desires.

You might say, "I am so lonely, and I want a boyfriend!" My response is that is a warning sign. Dive into God and build a relationship with him before you take anyone else who comes along.

When it comes to relationships, I love this saying: "You must be so busy doing God's work that God has to interrupt you to tell you he has someone special for you." Isn't that powerful?

Give God your desire to have that relationship. Focus on what God's desire is for you by praying, going to church, and being used by God to bring others to know him.

Prayer always steers you the right way. When you want to know if that relationship is right for you, pray. God will show you in your heart. You will just have that feeling. The more you pray, the more you will know God's voice tugging at your heart. It might be a feeling inside that you recognize, or maybe he will speak to your heart through Scripture.

When I went through lonely times, I would just dive into the Word. I would keep myself so busy with God's work that I didn't have time to dwell on being the only girl without a boyfriend. Before I knew it, I was so over that crazy feeling of needing a guy to fulfill me that all I wanted to do was help others get closer to God.

Your high school years are a great time to hang out with a group of friends who love God. Set up times for you all to go out and eat at a restaurant and have some clean fun. Being around friends who believe like you do will be fulfilling. It will take your mind off yourself and put the focus on God.

God, Use Me

When I was a teenager, I would ask God to use me. "Here I am Lord. Send me." It is like I was in a classroom, raising my hand to God and saying, "Please use me." I prayed that God would connect me with kids who were lonely and just needed someone to show God to them.

I can guarantee that once you ask God to use you, he will! I decided that I didn't have to be a youth pastor to be used by God. I could go out and bring others into the youth group. It didn't take but maybe a week, and God started showing me hurting guys and girls who needed to be encouraged.

I prayed over many to receive Jesus into their hearts. I would just ask them if they wanted to rededicate their lives to God. I figured I might never see them again, and I might be the only person ever to ask them that question. I would then lead them in a prayer and get them going with God. I reached out to others and gave them books to read. I made them Christian music tracks to listen to that would help them get on the right track. Whatever kept me focused on God, I shared with others.

God will use you—in your school, at your age, right now.

Taking On Positions of Influence

I became the Fellowship of Christian Athletes president and was very active getting the word out to join the group. Pastor JP was our support and helped us in our meetings. Many kids got closer to God during those meetings, and the fellowship gave us a platform to share our faith.

If you get a chance to run for the student government or any other positions at school, I encourage you to build your confidence up and go for it. God will use you in supernatural ways to change lives.

Praying Over the Lockers at School

Do you remember how I prayed over the lockers? God did begin to move across the campus. At that time, there were I Love Jesus pins, and it became a fad to wear those pins on our shirts. I had kids from all grades asking me for a pin. This went on for a couple of months.

You might say, "Well, those kids just wore the pin because everyone else was wearing it." And yeah, you might be right. But God used that simple act of wearing a pin to cause something special to happen across that school.

That pin might have reminded someone to go back to a youth group or maybe to read the Bible again. You will never know the impact that something that simple might have. When God says do it, you obey. He will do the rest.

Bringing a Revival to your School

God brought another revival at my daughter's high school. A group of about twelve kids who named themselves the G Force or God Force prayed that God would cause kids to want him. The G Force consisted of sophomores and juniors. Just using these kids, Pastor JP and I saw a revival break out among the students. The pastor said he had never seen anything quite like this.

The revival started out meeting at my house for a few hours every Sunday night. They had leader who would come each week. They would pray over their school and talk about whom they could get to come to the next meeting. The kids were football players, cheerleaders, band members, soccer players, basketball players—you name it, they were coming. It was a mixture of all denominations coming together to be a part of something, to connect with others who were trying to live for God. The leaders brought more kids every week. We grew from twenty-five to fifty and all the way to eighty-five kids who attended for several weeks.

As athletes, God had given the leaders a voice to use in the schools. They created a Facebook page. My daughter took pictures of them, and throughout the evening the students played games and posted the pictures. The students went out in the field near my house to play kickball or whiffle ball. After we played games, we ate dinner and then got deep into God's Word. Over five hundred friends kept watch online over what we did every Sunday night.

It only takes a few committed kids to start a revival. I encourage you to go after your school for God. A few of you can get together and start something very special that will overtake your school. Get with your youth pastor and let him know that you want to start a revival at your school. Get your friends together, pray, and ask God what he wants you to do.

Questions on Prayer:

Take time to ask yourself these questions. Ask God to help you. Be strong as you make a stand for God.

* Are you praying daily?

* Do you have a set prayer time?

* Have you prayed about the relationship you are in now and whether your relationship is right for you?

* Have you prayed for new friends?

* Are you praying for God to use you?

* Are you comfortable praying to God?

Fuel Stop:

Do you spend time worshipping God before you pray?

Read Psalm 100 and see how we are to come into God's presence. Try singing to God on your own. Just make up songs about him, letting him know how much you appreciate him. Do this before you start asking God for anything.

Ask God to speak to you. Now is the time for you to really seek God and pray over your life.

Ask God to use you to reach out to others and to change their lives. Maybe God wants to use you to start a revival at your school.

Scripture verses to think about:

So then do not be foolish, but understand what the Lord's will is. (Ephesians 5:17 NIV).

So, I say to you; Ask and it will be given to you; seek and you will find; knock and the door will be opened to you (Luke 11:9 NIV).

Trust in the Lord with all your heart and lean not on your own understanding; in all your ways submit to him, and he will make your paths straight. (Proverbs 3:5 NIV).

Look to the Lord and his strength; Seek his face always (Psalms 105:4 NIV).

Surely God is my salvation; I will trust and not be afraid. The Lord, the Lord himself, is my strength and my defense; he has become my salvation. (Isaiah 12:2 NIV)

Chapter 4

CHURCH

Insights from Chantell

I remember the first time I was invited to a youth group by my new friend. It was called Friday Night Lights. There was a full youth service with an activity, like a softball game, after service.

I was excited and finally feeling a part of something that I could call mine. I went every Friday night. At first I looked forward to playing whatever sport they had scheduled. I didn't care to hear what Pastor JP preached, but I really looked forward to the game.

After about a month, something happened. I now wanted more of God. I started looking forward to hearing what Pastor JP would speak about. I got excited about reading my Bible, and most of all about bringing others to know God.

I think it's important to become a part of a youth group because it gets you around others who think like you do. They go through struggles like you do. You can share with each other how you feel and maybe even encourage others by talking about how you are moving forward with God. Going to a youth group keeps you refreshed so that you can be reminded of God's desires for your life.

It was not long after I started that I decided I wanted to be a leader in my youth group. I wanted to learn how to disciple others and help them grow in God. Soon I was ready to tell others about how God could change their lives.

I brought many to church. My little yellow car would hold four or five kids. Every Friday night I would get youth group kids and bring them to church. My brother, three years younger, was in high school with me. We brought his friends to church as well.

I couldn't forget about my own family. My brother was my priority. God spoke to my heart and said, "If you can't get along with your brother and help him grow in God, then how can you expect to bring others to me?"

So many times I see youth run from their brothers and sisters instead of reaching out to them. Brothers and sisters need a family member to bring them to church. Youths need to help their own siblings get close to God.

As I reached out to my brother, we reached out to his friends. Before long, I had many lives to check on every week to make sure they had not gotten off track with God. If they had, well, I would pump them up again and encourage them to come to church and to defeat the Devil.

I tell my kids every day to go out and be the church. We are going into places that our pastors can't go, and so we are to bring the people we find there into the church. Galatians 6:9 (ASV) says, "And let us not be weary in well-doing: for in due season we shall reap, if we faint not."

Go Out and Get Your Friends

There are many of your friends who need you. They may have lost their way and need you to help them get back on track.

Recently I was speaking with a young football player who has a huge calling on his life. He had been spreading the Word of God in the hallways of his school. Then one day he felt himself slipping into a rut. At the time I first spoke to him, he said he couldn't get out of it.

I told him to stand by his bed and take a step forward. As he took that step, he would be making a declaration to God: "I am moving forward and not turning back." I also told him to say, "Devil, get behind me in the name of Jesus!"

He did it. As he repeated the words and took that step forward, he said he felt a huge weight lift off of him. He felt free.

I think sometimes the Devil paralyzes us. We forget to read our Bibles and forget to go to church. It starts out slowly. Maybe you forget to do your devotion and to pray one day. Then two days. Before you know it, you have not prayed in a week. Or maybe you play sports and have long practices after school. You get tired and have a hard time staying focused.

One way or another, you find yourself in a rut. You have to really push yourself not to forget God's word. Keep yourself in church. The Devil knows if he can distract you and cause you to forget him, he can send you on a totally different path than the path God intended. You will get weak and find yourself compromising. You might say, "Well, if I go to this party, I won't do anything. I'll just hang out with everyone."

I tell youth not to put themselves in a situation where they might be tempted to make a wrong choice. Especially if you have not been reading your Bible or going to church, your "God senses" are not in full force. You aren't as sharp to see the Devil's tricks as you would have been if you were focusing on God.

I remind my kids daily to get in the Word and speak their confessions over their lives. It brings protection over them as they go to school.

1 Peter 5:8 (AB) says, "Be well balanced (temperate, sober of mind), be vigilant and cautious at all times; for that enemy of yours, the devil, roams around like a lion roaring [in fierce hunger], seeking someone to seize upon and devour."

Let's break this down for moment. It says "be vigilant and cautious at all times," meaning stay focused on God, stay in the Word, and go to church. That is being vigilant. Being cautious means to always keep your head up, staying prepared in case the enemy tries to sidetrack you. Never let your guard down.

Being a Soldier in the Army of God

Every morning you go to school, you are going into a war zone. You are a soldier in the army of God. Your goal is to destroy the Devil's works. As Scripture says, you have to be ready and cautious at all times.

You can use texting to invite friends to church and to send them an encouraging word. Social media is an incredible way to check on your friends to help them stay focused.

Send group texts to let your friends know you are going to youth group, and share what you will be doing to encourage them to come with you. It's a great way to keep them out of the rut.

Insights from Pastor JP

When I was a young boy, we moved from the city to the country. After a while we settled into the slower rural lifestyle, and we started collecting animals. I say "collecting" because we never set out to find these animals.

Dogs would strangely appear at our house. A local farmer brought me a truckload of piglets who were runts of their litters. The farmer said he didn't have time to care for them, and they would die without special attention. So I became the surrogate mother of a bunch of pigs. My grandfather unexpectedly brought us a horse he picked up at a sale. Before long, I was Dr. Doolittle (the movie veterinarian who talks with the animals).

I soon realized that with every animal came more work for me, something that was never explained to me up front. I had just assumed animals took care of themselves, like a battery-operated type of thing. I learned this was not the case. I had undeservedly become their daily savior, sustainer, provider, and deliverer. If I didn't respond to their needs, they would not last long.

I never had a day off. I could never say to my dog Midnight, "Hey, I'm going out of town a few weeks. See ya when I get back." No sir, those animals only survived to the degree I showed my love to them. In other words, my title of "animal savior" came at a cost.

I'm like that animal on the farm. I can't sustain myself without help from God and the local church. I was designed to live in a community of people, and that's how this thing called "the local church" works.

The local church is the thing that feeds me and gives me daily sustenance. It's the tool God uses not only to keep me in the game, but to sharpen my spiritual skill set as well.

The local church gives you nourishment.

Not long ago, a friend of mine began to experience kidney failure. The doctors told him he had two choices. The first was to do nothing, live life, and plan his funeral. Not a very exciting option in my opinion. Option two was to hook himself up to a dialysis machine a couple times a week and live. He took option two.

It's the same way with church. Church is your spiritual dialysis machine. It's the tool designed by God to keep your insides clean and healthy, to edify you and build you up.

The Local Church as Spiritual Gym

I took up weight lifting years ago as a way to stay fit and found that the church is like my spiritual gym. It keeps me toned spiritually. It's not God's only tool he uses to keep us in shape spiritually, but it is the main tool.

In fact, the Bible tells us that Jesus came and died for the church. That's interesting to me because the church hadn't even been instituted yet. It was just a concept in the mind of Christ that would only find its manifestation once Jesus died on the cross.

You see, the moment Jesus screamed "It is finished," from the cross in his last dying breath, *boom*! The earth literally shook from an earthquake, and the old way of worship ended. Killing animals and begging God for forgiveness were no longer the ways we would seek God. God was ending something old and worn out to initiate a brand-new thing so powerful it would affect the entire world.

When Jesus exploded out of that tomb three days later, no one had a clue that we were only fifty days away from another supernatural birth. It was a birth that eclipsed any birthing story told by a woman at some afternoon tea. It was the birth of the church.

Ever since Jesus had started his ministry just three years before, he had been working on a plan. It was a totally foreign concept to us, but something that had been in his heart for eons of time. It was the local church.

Jesus even gave the disciples a clue to what was on his mind when he told them, "Upon this rock [by which he meant himself], I will build my church."

Being Used by God

What am I talking about when I mention the local church? I'm talking about a group of born-again believers who consistently meet together to worship, sing, praise, encourage each other, and train to become ministers themselves.

Wait a minute, did I say "minister"? You, a minister? Yes. In fact, every single Christian must strive to develop him or herself into an adequate minister of the word. Not that you will be preaching from a big Bible and wearing a black robe while standing behind a pulpit anytime soon—or at all. But you will be a person who stands for something, a bold person who has begun to live with a sense of purpose.

You have a knowing inside of you that God has put you on this earth at this time, for this moment, for this generation, and with a task to accomplish. You will become a person who lives each day like a missionary in your own town.

In the Bible, the apostle Paul says we are to live like foreigners or strangers in the land. (1 Peter 2:11 NIV) In other words, we're really not part of this world even though we live here. We go to school, and if we are really hungering after God, it's as if we are strangers. We don't seem to fit in. Those cruel jokes about the unpopular kids just don't do anything for us anymore. Why? Because we've been changed!

What you need now is to surround yourself as often as you can with people just like you. You need the church. In fact, the word church actually means "the called-out ones," the people who realize they no longer think and act as others do. In a sense, they've been called out of all that stuff in the world.

The Church Is Like a Family

Studying the Bible, you will find that it likens the church to an army, bride, city, and body. My favorite comparison, though, is that of the church as a family.

Everybody wants to have or be in a family. I remember being the chaplain of one of the largest juvenile detention facilities on the East Coast. I never met a kid in that huge jail who said he didn't want to be a part of a family. Even if he never really had an opportunity to be in one, he still longed for it.

There's nothing better than being part of a family that is doing it right. Think about it. Your family is where you learn how to eat, have manners (hopefully), and be responsible (yes, you need to clean your room and take out the trash). It prepares you to live in the real world. A family allows you to fail, mess up, fall flat on your face, and still be loved and accepted. In the family, you learn how selfish you are (no, that's *my* cookie) and hopefully how to give, share, and prefer one another.

I recently was coaching my son's basketball team, and we had a boy playing who had never played before. In fact, he didn't enjoy sports at all and had never ventured into the sports world. However, his sister was very athletic and was a very good soccer player. He loved and adored her. One day I asked him why he had waited this long to begin playing sports. He told me it was because he loved his sister so much. I nodded my head, said "oh," and let it drop.

Later his mother told me that his sister had died in a tragic car accident the year before. He had loved her so much that he decided he would play sports for her. He confided to me that every time he played, he felt he was making her smile.

That is family love.

Not long ago, I heard that a child needed a kidney and the only match was her brother. The boy begged his parents to let him donate his organ to save his sister's life.

That is family love.

This is what happens when you're in a family or a church. It becomes a place where you gain access to the incredible depth of God's love. It just happens. You start looking at people in the church as precious people that you're absolutely in love with. It is here, in this setting, that it begins to dawn on you that real life comes from giving and not getting. After a while, all you want to do is give of yourself to help them become all that they were meant to be.

In the Church You Discover Your Gifts

It's in the church, just like in the family, that you discover your gifts. I've always enjoyed singing and was in the choir in school. But it never dawned on me that singing was something God could use—not until I started attending a great youth group. Every week we had a youth service complete with a youth band, and the worship was always led by a couple of young people who could sing.

One day I happened to say without thinking to a friend of mine that "I could do that." I said it without expecting anyone to hear me. My friend asked what I had said, and I said, "Nothing, I was just talking to myself." He kept after me until I spilled the beans and told him I had this wild thought that I could be a worship leader. He told me to ask the youth pastor to allow me the opportunity. I argued, but thankfully he persisted. That's what church family does, I found out.

Finally I worked up the courage to tell the youth pastor that if he ever needed another leader, then I would be willing to lead the worship. Totally unexpectedly, he said, "Fine. You will lead this Friday."

I said, "No, I didn't mean right away," but it was too late. He had already walked off.

Well, sure enough, I led the worship service that Friday and it was a train wreck. All I can say was it couldn't be over fast enough. Have you ever had one of those moments when you did something so horribly that not only did you feel mortified, but everyone in the room was embarrassed for you. I might as well been standing there with my zipper down for thirty minutes.

That weekend at church, I knew I had to apologize to the youth pastor for being so arrogant as to think I could lead worship, and ask him to forgive me for ruining the service.

When he walked into the room I was in, I grabbed him and made my confession. His response? "Not a problem, man. You're leading again this Friday."

I said, "What?" Had he not heard me? Was he not present at the last meeting? Had he lost his mind? I was stunned. I was mortified. I had proven I could not lead the worship, and now he was asking me to do it again.

Great, I thought. I had put myself directly in front of the firing squad, and when this thing was over, I would have no self-respect, no self-esteem, and no friends. My life was ruined.

And my friend who had encouraged me to begin just kept encouraging me to do it again. I thought the whole place was losing its collective mind.

So I led the worship service again the next week with great fear and trembling—and this time it was okay. Not a five-star experience, but definitely not a disaster.

After that the youth pastor put me in the regular rotation. I was now a certified worship leader, even though each time I got up to lead I felt as if I were walking on the edge of a cliff, about to fall off at any moment.

As it turned out, I continued to lead for years after that and found myself flowing in a genuine ministry God had designed me for. Thankfully I had an incredible church family. Without their encouragement and belief in God's gift in me, I never would have stepped into my calling and purpose.

Do you see how important it is to be a part of a church family?

Lastly, you will find that the church will offer you an opportunity to die to yourself. The church is one of the main ways God allows us to put others first, a concept totally opposed and foreign to the society we live in.

Elisha the Prophet

One day I was reading about how the prophet Elisha got his start. You have to understand the background of Elisha's life to really appreciate how he became one of the most powerful men on the earth in his time.

Elisha, the future prophet, grew up on a farm. His father had undoubtedly gained quite a bit of land, which required lots of people to do the plowing. This included Elisha on the day he was discovered. The infamous prophet Elijah, who had declared there would be no rain for three years, came walking by that day. He spotted Elisha and must have heard the Lord speak to him that this man could be his replacement.

So Elijah went to the young Elisha in the field and informed him that God had his hand on Elisha's life. If Elisha wanted to be used by God, the decision was his. Immediately, with no explanation of what that meant or would look like, Elijah walked off.

Elisha had a good thing going there with his dad. He was destined to inherit a successful farm, and life could have been good for him. But then there was this thing that had just happened. The most powerful man on earth had said Elijah had the potential for more.

Then the most amazing thing happened. Contrary to what a normal person would have done, Elisha burned his plow, killed his oxen, and took off after Elijah. To do what? Serve. Elisha would wait on Elijah hand and foot. He did whatever he could do to make Elijah's life easier. He did this for years. There's no record of any complaining, whining, or murmuring, just serving, day in and day out.

Elijah the great prophet did seven miracles in his lifetime. Then when it was time for him to leave this earth, he asked his faithful servant Elisha what he could do for him. Elisha replied, "Give me a double portion." In other words I want twice as much as you.

Guess what? By the time Elisha was ready to die, he had performed fourteen miracles. This was twice as many as Elijah had performed.

When I read that story, I knew the Lord was showing me something. He was telling me that if I ever wanted to be great, if I ever wanted to be used mightily, then it must come through the tool of servanthood. I would have to learn to become a servant.

"But how?" I asked myself.

It would be through the local church family.

That was it. I purposefully set out to become the greatest servant in our church. Not that there was some kind of contest going on, but if there was one, at least I wanted to be in the running.

That, my friend, was one of the greatest things that ever happened to me. I quickly died to my desires and put others before myself. I signed up for every workday. I picked up kids on the other side of town and gave rides to church using my own car and gas. I volunteered to babysit my youth pastor's kids on multiple occasions. (That was scary.)

The point is, I just gave myself away. It became a lifestyle, and I was changed. The Lord had used the church family as his tool to change me. I'm not so sure if the Lord needs me or if the church needs me, but I have learned that I desperately need him and the church. So do you.

It's time you set your mind to becoming a servant. It really is a modern-day term. It's not a bad thing but a great thing when you become God's servant and lay your life down for the church. You change. You can't help it, it just happens. You actually become a loving and compassionate person. Don't you want to become that? Sure you do.

Questions on church:

Take time to ask yourself these questions. Ask God to help you. Be strong as you make a stand for God.

* Do I attend church regularly?

* Do I encourage others to come to my youth group?

* How can I make a difference in my youth group?

* Do I work at bringing my brothers and sisters to youth group?

Fuel Stop:

Find a local church that you look forward to attending and that challenges you to grow in spiritual matters. Pray and ask God if this is your church family. Listen to the answer.

If God shows you that this is your church family, ask the minister what you have to do to join it. Then join it. Commit to it.

Start serving today, even if that is not what you particularly enjoy doing. You then will find your place in the church family.

Remember, everybody has a family and a certain role to play in that family. Find someone in the church family who is a little older and a little wiser than you, and ask that person to train you in the things of God. Turn around and do the same for someone else.

Scripture verses to think about:

Let us not become weary in doing good, for at the proper time we will reap a harvest if we do not give up. (Galatians 6:9 NIV).

Finally, be strong in the Lord and in his mighty power. (Ephesians 6:10 NIV).

And having disarmed the powers and authorities, he made a public spectacle of them, triumphing over them by the cross. (Colossians 2:15 NIV).

I have given you authority to trample on snakes and scorpions and to overcome all the power of the enemy; nothing will harm you. (Luke 10:19 NIV).

Be alert and of sober mind. Your enemy the devil prowls around like a roaring lion looking for someone to devour. (1Peter 5:8 NIV)

Notes

CPSIA information can be obtained at www.ICGtesting.com
Printed in the USA
LVOW040719120912

298406LV00001B/3/P